C000182741

LICHFIELD
THEN & NOW
IN COLOUR

ANNETTE RUBERY

The
History
Press

In memory of my father, Peter.

First published in 2012

The History Press
The Mill, Brimscombe Port
Stroud, Gloucestershire, GL5 2QG
www.thehistorypress.co.uk

© Annette Rubery, 2012

The right of Annette Rubery to be identified as the Author
of this work has been asserted in accordance with the
Copyrights, Designs and Patents Act 1988.

British Library Cataloguing in Publication Data.
A catalogue record for this book is available from the British Library.

ISBN 978 0 7524 6113 7

Typesetting and origination by The History Press
Printed in India.

CONTENTS

ACKNOWLEDGEMENTS

Many people have helped me with the words and images in this book. My biggest thanks are due to my partner, Richard Bratby, who not only gave me his expertise and advice (the railway captions in particular benefit from his detailed knowledge), he also helped me to source the old photographs – a task that involved travelling to all manner of postcard and ephemera fairs up and down the country. He has also forfeited many of his Sunday afternoons to help me carry my photographic kit around Lichfield, pored over websites and old maps, and helped me to match each photograph to the landscape with his sharp eye for detail. Above all, he kept me going with words of common-sense and encouragement. Thank you so much, Richard.

I am also indebted to Joanne Wilson, Museums and Heritage Officer at The Samuel Johnson Birthplace Museum, who gave me permission to reproduce the photographs on p.15, p.35, p.48, p.52, p.55 and p.56, and also assisted me with the captions for 'Varney's' splendid photograph of the Johnson Birthplace Museum and the statue of King Edward VII. I would also like to thank fellow History Press author Mark Norton, for his kind permission to reproduce the railway photographs on p.70 and p.73 (both of which were taken by his father, Dennis John Norton), and Bob Williams of the Lichfield and Hatherton Canals Restoration Trust, for providing the photograph on p.61. I am also grateful to David Wallington and his team at Lichfield Heritage Centre for permission to reproduce the photographs on p.16, p.30, p.40, p.75, p.76 and p.80, and to photographer Robert Yardley, for his generosity in providing the very fine modern picture of the Lichfield Bower on p.34.

Warm thanks are also due to Mr and Mrs Gingell, Madeleine Budgen, Michael Mullarkey, Peter Young, Fran Ambrose, Phil Davies, Gareth Hare, Helen Jones, Alison Ivens, Jenny Arthur, Louise and Margaret Thompson, the staff at the Lichfield Record Office, Kate Gomez, Vickie Sutton, the staff at The Staffordshire Regiment Museum, and to my mother, Rita Rubery, all of whom offered support, information and help of many different kinds. Last but not least I want to thank my editor, Matilda Richards, for her unwavering patience with my many emails.

INTRODUCTION

St Chad was among the first to recognise the potential of Lichfield, when he came to the kingdom of Mercia to establish his monastery in the seventh century. Since then, the small city in Staffordshire has experienced a civil war; had its cathedral destroyed and rebuilt; witnessed the birth of the great antiquarian Elias Ashmole, and that of Samuel Johnson, author of the first scholarly English dictionary. It has nurtured the Georgian period's greatest actor, David Garrick; welcomed Erasmus Darwin, who offered the first glimpse of a new theory of evolution; and inspired any number of poets and authors.

Although one of the smallest English cathedral cities, Lichfield has a rich history – partly due to its importance as an ecclesiastical centre, but also because of its central location just north of Birmingham, at the crossroads of two important trunk routes. During the Civil War it found itself on the borderline between Loyalist and Parliamentary sympathisers, and its medieval cathedral, with its fortified walls and turrets, was soon in the firing line. Yet despite all this, Lichfield rallied, entering the eighteenth century as a genteel city, bolstered by the coaching trade which brought wealthy visitors from across the country. Much of the architecture of that period has been carefully preserved, and continues to give the city its character.

Unsurprisingly for a garrison city, Lichfield was never short of public houses and was known nationwide for the quality of its beer. Therefore, pubs crop up quite a lot in this book. One reason for the quality of its ale could have been Lichfield's excellent supplies of fresh water. Lichfield lies in a valley, fed by several streams, which have in turn created shallow pools and boggy ground known locally as moggs. Minster Pool and Stowe Pool lie south and east of the cathedral, and before the eighteenth century there was a third pool, where the Museum Gardens now stand. Daniel Defoe, visiting Lichfield in the 1720s, observed that Minster Pool 'parts Lichfield, as it were, into two cities, one is call'd the town, and the other the close'. Lichfield has always been divided by these bodies of water, both physically and psychologically, with 'town and gown' having their own distinct traditions. The Close has seen its times of trouble, but today it is the town that stands at the forefront of development, and has responded with customs of its own: the Samuel Johnson birthday celebrations and the Greenhill Bower.

The biggest challenge posed by *Lichfield Then & Now* has not been what to include, but what to omit. I have tried to source pictures of all the familiar landmarks – the cathedral, the pools, the old coaching inns – but I have also searched for Lichfield's forgotten heritage: its splendid eighteenth-century mansion Beacon Place; the Victoria Hospital; the old racecourse stand on Whittington Heath, and the Lichfield branch of the Wyrley and Essington Canal. It is tempting to imagine that historic Lichfield never changes, but while working on this book I have been surprised to observe how even the most obvious landmarks have altered in subtle ways. I hope that the reader will share my pleasure in tracking the passage of time through the photographs in this book, and even, perhaps, begin to see Lichfield with new eyes. As Dr Johnson shrewdly observed, 'To judge rightly of the present, we must oppose it to the past; for all judgment is comparative, and of the future nothing can be known.'

Annette Rubery, 2012

BEACON HILL

BEACON STREET (OR Bacon Street, as it was written prior to 1836) was once the principal street of Lichfield, and, because of its proximity to the cathedral, sustained a fair amount of damage during the Civil War. The raised ground of Beacon Hill, being the highest point north of the cathedral, was used by both Royalist and Parliamentary troops at different stages of the conflict as an ideal place from which to attack, or simply to observe, the enemy (the view shown on this early twentieth-century postcard is not far from the gun emplacement earthworks, still known today as Prince Rupert's Mount). Here we are looking downhill towards an area known as New Town during the Victorian period. This small community developed around a foundry, opened by

Walsall firm Chamberlin & Hill in 1890 on the junction between Beacon Street and Grange Lane (now Wheel Lane). The foundry (marked as Phoenix Foundry on the 1921 map) was eventually demolished to make way for a supermarket. (Author's collection)

WITH THE EXCEPTION of the modern street furniture, you can see that Beacon Hill still retains much of its former character. The grand timber-framed building on the right is a mix of periods, though bits of it seem to date from the late seventeenth or early eighteenth century. Because Beacon Street was such a major road in and out of the city (and still, in fact, forms the route of the ancient Sheriff's Ride), it has always had more than its fair share of pubs. According to John Shaw in *The Old Pubs of Lichfield*, The Pheasant operated on Beacon Hill from 1861 until about 1909, and the building (now a private residence) still stands, just out of shot to the left of the photograph. Further down the hill was The Lemon Tree, which Shaw says was listed in 1834 and appears to have closed in 1915, probably as a result of the war (this building also still survives). Three reasonably historic pubs that are still in operation on this road are The George and Dragon, The Feathers and The Fountain.

CATHEDRAL CLOSE

THIS LOMAS & SON photograph shows a much-loved view of the cathedral from the entrance to the Close on Beacon Street. It was Bishop Walter de Langton (1296-1321) who was responsible for walling the Close for 'the honour of God, the dignity of the Cathedral, and the bodies of the saints there reposing, and also for security and quiet of the canons'. If you look at this view today, just out of shot of this photograph on the left-hand side, you can still see the remains of the masonry belonging to Langton's West Gate, which, despite the slighting of all the fortifications around the Close after the Civil War, was left standing until 1800, when, along with the coach house that adjoined No. 24 and part of a house in the ditch, it was demolished to make way for the building of Newton's College (the imposing building on the right). Designed by Joseph Potter the elder, the college was founded by Andrew Newton (the son of a Lichfield brandy merchant) as an almshouse for the widows and unmarried daughters of the clergy. (Author's collection)

THE CONTEMPORARY PHOTOGRAPH shows how, visually at least, very little has changed. Because of the lack of eligible residents, Newton's College ceased to be an almshouse in 1988, when the college trustees transferred the building to the Dean and Chapter. The college, along

with an additional building (also designed by Joseph Potter) at the south-west corner of the range in Beacon Street, is now used as rental housing. In July every year, the Cathedral Close bustles with visitors to the Lichfield Festival – a multi-art-form event founded in 1981 by John Lang and Gordon Clark. Among the community activities on offer is a particularly unusual one called the Cathedral Dash, which has taken place here since 1998. As the cathedral bells chime noon on the appointed day, athletes race around the cathedral in a recreation of the famous quadrangle scene from the film *Chariots of Fire*. The timber-framed building on the left-hand-side of this photograph, nearest to the west front of the cathedral, now houses the Lichfield Festival office.

LICHFIELD FREE LIBRARY AND MUSEUM

THE FREE LIBRARY and Museum stands at the end of Bird Street, near to the west front of cathedral, and close to the foundations of an ancient tower. Nikolaus Pevsner, in his guide to Staffordshire, dismisses it as 'small, of yellow brick and funny', yet this building – designed by Bidlake & Lovatt and built between 1857 and 1859 – was an important symbol of Victorian civic pride. Thanks to the Public Libraries Act of 1850, which made funding available to municipal corporations, Lichfield became the second city in Britain to erect a public library (the first was Manchester). Chancellor Thomas James Law was one of the project's champions, and laid the

foundation stone on 3 October 1857 to the strains of Haydn's *Creation*. There is a curious statue of a Boer War-era sailor on the side of the building; this was originally created for a war memorial in York, but was later rejected on the grounds that it was *too* warlike (the usual conventions were to show soldiers helping the wounded or remembering their comrades, rather than armed and ready to fight). The statue was given to Lichfield by the sculptor Robert Bridgeman in 1905. (Author's collection)

WHEN YOU CONSIDER that the builders – Messrs Lilley of Wolverhampton – made the mistake of building the Free Library and Museum partly on sandstone rock and partly on silt, it is a miracle that this building has survived. Given the notoriously marshy ground here (in medieval times it was the site of the Bishop's Fish Pool, and later became waterlogged marshland known as Swan Moggs), it wasn't long before the south-west corner began to sink. The ugly buttresses that you can see in both photographs were added to the sides of the structure, but the problem wasn't satisfactorily solved until the whole building was underpinned by steel girders in 1938. The museum must have been quite something in its day (in 1874 John Hewitt boasted that it had every kind of object, 'from an Athenian temple to a lady's needle case'), but by 1958 it had vacated the premises, and by 1989 – when the eastern end of the Friary was converted into a public library and record office – its days as a library were also numbered. Today, the building is occupied by Lichfield Register Office.

MUSEUM GARDENS, BEACON PARK

IN THE EARLY nineteenth century, Lichfield's water supply from Aldershawe was found to be
diminishing, and various suggestions were put forth by the South Staffordshire Waterworks
Company to rectify the problem. The side-effect of one scheme would have involved filling in
Minster Pool and building public gardens in its place, complete with an ornamental fountain, but
this so enraged the citizens of Lichfield that the idea was dropped. The company's subsequent plan,
which involved building a network of tunnels and well-shafts to carry water from Leomansley and
Trunkfield Brooks into Stowe Pool, was approved, however, and the leftover soil was used to lay out
the Museum Gardens, which were officially opened in 1859. The ornamental fountain by Turner

and Allen of London (a gift from 'one-man civic society', Chancellor Law) was unveiled in 1871, while the Band of the Staffordshire Militia played Handel's *Water Music*. You can see the fountain, surrounded by couchant lions, in this postcard dating from the early 1900s. (Author's collection)

ONE OF THE most obvious additions to this view of the Museum Gardens, taken in 2011, is the statue of King Edward VII, which was unveiled in 1908 as a symbol of the city's loyalty to the King (this statue was the first of its kind to be erected in the country after the King's accession in 1901). In the old photograph, the other side of Bird Street is walled, whereas the new photograph shows how the area has been opened up with the construction of the Garden of Remembrance in 1920. It also shows the King's statue looking as good as new, following restoration work as part of the Historic Parks Project (the stone balustrade also had to be restored after being damaged in a car accident). Lichfield Conduit Lands Trust – an ancient body, founded in 1545 to safeguard Lichfield's water supply and the wellbeing of its citizens – gave £2,978 towards the restoration of Chancellor Law's fountain, which has an ornate basin decorated with herons, fish and reeds.

STATUE OF
KING EDWARD VII

THIS PHOTOGRAPH SHOWS a packed Museum Gardens during the unveiling of the statue of Edward VII (a gift to the city by the sculptor and then-Sheriff, Robert Bridgeman) on 30 September 1908. Sculpted from Portland Stone by George Lowther, the statue shows the King in full coronation robes, with collar, ribbon and star of the Order of the Garter, and with the sceptre in his right hand. On the front of the pedestal is the Imperial crown, and below that, the arms of the City of Lichfield on a shield. The following is typed on the mount to the photograph:

'Copy of Telegram. O.H.M.S. Balmoral Castle. The Mayor of Lichfield, Town Hall, Lichfield, October 1st 1908. The King commands me to thank you for your telegram giving account of proceedings at unveiling of His statue yesterday and to say that His Majesty greatly appreciated the good feeling and Loyalty shewn on the occasion. Knollys'. 'Copy of Letter, Balmoral Castle. The Private Secretary is commanded by the King to thank the Mayor of Lichfield and to say that His Majesty has much pleasure in accepting it.'

(Samuel Johnson Birthplace Museum)

THE MODERN PHOTOGRAPH shows the King's statue standing amongst the flower beds, having recently been cleaned as part of the Historic Parks Project. Since 1914, King Edward VII has been joined in the Museum Gardens by a statue of the Captain of the *Titanic*, Commander Edward John Smith, sculpted by Lady Kathleen Scott (the widow of Antarctic explorer Captain Robert Scott). The official explanation for Captain Smith's presence is that Lichfield is at the centre of the diocese in which he was born, but some maintain that the sculpture was in fact rejected by the people of his birthplace, Hanley. Over the years the Museum Gardens have also housed a Crimean War cannon and a First World War German gun, but they were removed, along with many of the city's railings, for scrap metal for the war effort in 1940. For many years the model for the King's statue was stored at Robert Bridgeman's workshop on Quonians Lane (see p.80), but in 1968 it was destroyed by workmen renovating the building.

BEACON PLACE

BEACON PLACE – WHICH stood in what is now Beacon Park – was built in the late eighteenth century by George Hand, a proctor of the consistory court. After his death in 1806, his widow Ann lived there until she died in 1826. The sales particulars of that year give us some idea of what the house was like; there was a library, a 'staircase of Hopton stone, lighted by an elegant skylight' and an excellent kitchen, while the grounds included a brew-house, wash-house and a kitchen garden, orchard, greenhouse, extensive hot-house 'well stacked with choice vines', and a pinery (a hot-house for growing pineapples). Not all of the estate was freehold; two areas (called Cock Croft and Upper Maudlin's Well) were leased by the Subchanter and Vicars Choral of the cathedral, while a third, called Cooper's Croft, was leased by the Dean and Chapter. In 1827, the property was sold to Lichfield attorney Thomas Hinckley, who, with his wife Ellen

Jane (the daughter of J.C. Woodhouse, Dean of Lichfield), turned it into a very up-market property. (Lichfield Heritage Collection)

THE OLD PHOTOGRAPH clearly shows one of the two wings (designed by Sydney Smirke) that were added to Beacon Place by the Hinckleys. Some of the opulence of the interior is summed up by the inventory of goods following Mrs Hinckley's death in 1870, which included fifty-eight oil paintings. The building – which, by now, stood in nearly 100 acres of land – passed to Arthur Hinckley (Richard's nephew), who sold it to Samuel Lipscombe Seckham, who in turn left it to his son Gerald on his death in 1901. During the First World War it was used as offices, and in the Second World War as a base for the Royal Army Service Corps. The house stood until 1964, when it was purchased by the council and demolished. Much of the grounds were incorporated into Beacon Park, but one piece (including Seckham Road, pictured above) was bought by a private developer who built houses on it. The position of the cathedral spires, just glimpsed through the trees, is one of the few remaining clues to where the 'then' photographer was standing.

LICHFIELD CATHEDRAL AND GARDEN OF REMEMBRANCE

THIS POSTCARD SHOWS a much-loved view, taken from the bridge in Bird Street, probably some time between the wars. Lichfield's pools have always been one of the city's chief beauties, but they have also been notoriously troublesome. Minster Pool, pictured here, was created in 1310 when Bishop Langton built a causeway across the expansive Middle Pool, but thanks to its sluggish water supply – and the sewage dumped into it by residents of the Cathedral Close – the water frequently silted up and overflowed its banks. Things improved briefly in the late eighteenth century, when the formidable local poet Anna Seward lobbied for Minster Pool to be cleaned and remodelled in the image of the Serpentine, but by the mid-nineteenth century local physician Dr James Rawson complained that: 'a lapse of 24 years has again brought [Minster Pool] to a state of exuberant filth!' It was only when the South Staffordshire Waterworks Company took over in 1853 that it finally achieved respectability. (Author's collection)

LICHFIELD'S GARDEN OF Remembrance was created in 1920 to commemorate the fallen of 1914-18. In 1937, Arthur Mee wrote in the *King's England* series of guidebooks that it is one of the 'most original and beautiful peace memorials in England'. This photograph was taken in 2010, shortly after the garden had been refurbished as part of the multi-million-pound Historic Parks Project (a partnership between Lichfield District Council and Lichfield City Council). The work involved restoring the war memorial, gates, lion statues, sundial and urns, and installing a new ramp and steps into the garden, along with relaying the paths and repairing the stone balustrade. According to Mee, the balustrade was removed from Moxhull Hall in Wishaw to Shenstone Court near Lichfield, before being bought by the city for use in this garden. While it was being installed it was discovered that one of the stones was marked with the letter V, used by the mason Vinrace. Coincidentally, Vinrace also built the bridge that crosses Minster Pool at this very spot.

THE SWAN, BIRD STREET

BIRD STREET WAS an important stopping-off place for Georgian travellers, housing as it did two major coaching inns: The Swan (which is the ivy-clad building on the right) and the George Hotel. No one really knows when The Swan was first established, but according to Howard Clayton and Kathleen Simmons in their book *The Lily-White Swan: A History of the Swan Hotel*, it is first mentioned in a document dated 1535, which describes it as standing 'at the end of the bridge'. (The bridge in question was the fourteenth-century structure that Bishop Langton built over Minster Pool, not the one in use today, which was designed by Joseph Potter in 1816.) The Swan has seen many famous visitors over the years; one source claims that the Duke of Cumberland stayed there in November 1745, en-route to crush the Jacobite uprising. The novelist George Eliot

reputedly visited three times. This postcard probably dates from 1905, when Lichfield's brand new post office (pictured on the left) had just opened. (Author's collection)

IN 1818, IT became apparent that Bird Street was too narrow to cope with the new, wheeled traffic of the coaching age and several houses were demolished opposite The Swan in order to widen the road. In modern times the redevelopment of Bird Street has continued with the introduction of the road which curves around to the left, providing access to a car park and Minster Pool Walk. Lichfield's post office, with its smart gabled roof, continued to function until a modern replacement was opened in the Bakers Lane precinct in 1968 (see p.74), and then the building lay derelict until 1970, when Lichfield City Council granted a license for its occupation as a temporary arts centre. By 1994, however, the enterprise was forced to close amidst claims that the building was subsiding. Today, New Minster House – built by BHB Architects to house luxury flats and a Mediterranean restaurant – stands in its place, though its striking white façade has raised some eyebrows amongst the locals.

THE GEORGE HOTEL, BIRD STREET

THIS 1923 POSTCARD of Bird Street is looking the other way up the street, in the direction of the Museum Gardens. The building on the right is an important Lichfield landmark – the George Hotel – whose history, like its neighbour, The Swan, is bound up with the eighteenth-century coaching trade. George Farquhar, the dramatist, remembered staying at the George (probably in those days a galleried coaching inn) in 1704, when he was serving in the Earl of Orrery's Regiment of Foot. The experience inspired his comedy *The Recruiting Officer*, which was penned, at least in part, on the George's premises. His final comedy, *The Beaux' Stratagem*, was actually set in Lichfield

and introduced popular comic figures such as Lady Bountiful and Staffordshire innkeeper, Boniface. The George's frontage seems to have been rebuilt in the late eighteenth century to include a central archway, giving access to the inn-yard beyond. In this picture you can still see the balcony over the archway, which was used by election candidates to address the masses. (Author's collection)

NOW PART OF the Best Western hotel chain, the George continues to welcome travellers. Even the ornate ballroom on the first floor is still in use (by local Regency dance enthusiasts, theatre companies and the Lichfield Literature Festival, among others). One important aspect of the George's history that no longer resonates today is its political allegiance; during the eighteenth and early nineteenth centuries it was strongly associated with the Whigs, whereas The Swan was favoured by the Tories. Each party met at its respective inn during election time – an arrangement that often ended in violence. Even the Prince Regent's visit to Lichfield after the Battle of Waterloo resulted in fisticuffs when it was discovered that the Royal horses had been supplied by The Swan, instead of the faithful Whigs at the George. These days Bird Street is lined with restaurants and bars, but its coaching history can still clearly be seen. The King's Head pub – just out of shot opposite the George – was once a coaching inn too, though much smaller than either of its neighbours.

SANDFORD STREET

THIS POSTCARD FROM around 1905 shows the view down Sandford Street, looking towards Bird Street. The Royal Oak inn is pictured in the foreground (its archway has a sign above it saying 'Good stabling'), while next door is The Old Brewery. The latter was built by the Griffith Brothers (see p.71) and later taken over by Davenport's Brewery as a distribution centre. Lichfield was always known for its breweries – an industry that probably flourished a result of the city's excellent water supply. In 1819, Charles Edward Stringer describes Sandford, or Sondeforde Street, as being divided into two parts by a brook, at which stood the city gates. He says: 'Sandford Street *intra bars* [within the gates], is in the parish of St Mary, *trans aquam* [across the water], in that of St Chad; a bridge was built over the brook about the year 1520.' Sandford Brook is clearly marked on John Snape's map of 1781, crossing what is now Lower Sandford Street. It was later re-named Trunkfield Brook, and is the same stream that meanders through the Festival Gardens today. (Author's collection)

SANDFORD STREET WAS an important medieval street, specialising in tanning, dyeing and cloth-making, and before the Friary was developed in the 1920s, it was the main route for traffic heading towards Walsall and Wolverhampton. Today it is less prominent, but the old buildings that have survived are an indication of its former status. This photograph was taken from what is now the junction with Swan Road. You can see that the Royal Oak has gone (it is thought to have closed some time between the wars) and the building across the road, with its bow-fronted window, has also disappeared, making way for a car park. Yet the two-storey attic house on the right (partly obscured by the lamppost) has survived and is thought to be a seventeenth-century structure with some nineteenth-century alterations. The timber-framed building further down on the same side of the street is now a bar and nightclub called The Paradise Lounge. The Old Brewery, on the left-hand side of the street, has had its top storey removed and is now an office building.

MARKET STREET

MARKET STREET – also known as Robe, Rox, Ross and Sadler Street – has been the centre of Lichfield trade for centuries, and this is reflected in its mixture of architectural styles, particularly at the western end. This photograph, taken about 1910 from the junction with Bird Street, shows an interesting mixture of eighteenth- and nineteenth-century buildings with W.J. Mercer's shop on the left and the Angel Inn on the right. The Angel, built around 1750, appears to have been a pub from at least 1800 but the building also incorporates a late nineteenth-century shop front, so it can't have traded exclusively in beer during its long history. A hairdresser's offering a scissor-sharpening service is next door. The Georgian name for this street, Saddler Street, indicates that leather was an important trade, and a close inspection of W.J. Mercer's sign reveals it to be a saddler and harness-maker. Built in 1780, with a superb bow-fronted window, the property still has its original carriageway giving access to what would have been the inn-yard of the George Hotel. Its cobbles are made from Rowley Rag: a volcanic stone quarried from the hills near to Rowley Regis in the West Midlands. (Author's collection)

AS HOWARD CLAYTON explains in *Coaching City*, the quality of the shop fronts in Market Street is a reflection of how closely work and home-life were intertwined during the Georgian period. As many shopkeepers lived in or above their place of work, the buildings incorporated high-quality design values though, in some cases, seventeenth-century timber-framed buildings were simply covered with ornate façades. This 2011 photograph shows that Lichfield's shop fronts are still very well preserved and the functions of the two buildings in the foreground even have an historic symmetry. The Angel Inn is still a pub, though the name was changed in the late 1970s to Samuel's in honour of Lichfield's famous son, Samuel Johnson. W.J. Mercer's shop – though no longer a saddler and harness-maker – in now occupied by Golunski, a company selling leather handbags and luggage. The former hairdresser across the road is now a jeweller. Out of sight on the left is another important Georgian shop front, Charrington's Pharmacy, which is now a branch of the fast-food chain Subway.

BORE STREET

IT IS NOT known where Bore Street got its name, but many sources agree that it refers to the boards used in the market to support goods and keep them off the muddy ground (just to confuse matters, several nineteenth-century guidebooks to Lichfield refer to it as Draper Street). As it is much wider than other Lichfield streets of the same period, it does appear to have been designed as the principal market street, although, over time, the market has gravitated elsewhere. On the left is Boswell House (now called The Tudor of Lichfield), a timber-framed building dated 1510 with three gables (see p.32). The buildings on the south side of the street appear much more uniform than those on the north, probably due to Georgian builders encasing

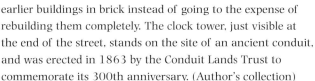

earlier buildings in brick instead of going to the expense of rebuilding them completely. The clock tower, just visible at the end of the street, stands on the site of an ancient conduit, and was erected in 1863 by the Conduit Lands Trust to commemorate its 300th anniversary. (Author's collection)

THE BUILDINGS REMAIN much the same today, although the structure nearest to the viewer on the right of the old photograph (a butcher's for many years, and, latterly, Crump's Ice Saloon) was demolished in the early 1930s. On the same side of the road, the tobacconist (displaying the Cigars sign) is now Cure clothing. The tall, white timber-framed house a couple of doors away is that of herbalist Dr China. Perhaps the most significant change to this view, however, is the removal of the clock tower at the end of the street. In the 1920s, the Friary estate was sold to Sir Richard Cooper, MP for Walsall, who gave it to the city for the purpose of redevelopment. Part of this work involved cutting a brand new road from the end of Bird Street – which had become a bottleneck for traffic – to the Walsall and Birmingham roads. The clock tower was initially marked out for demolition, but Sir Richard Cooper paid for it to be relocated south of the Festival Gardens, where it still stands today.

BORE STREET

BELIEVED TO DATE from around 1896, this photograph was taken from the corner of Bore Street and Breadmarket Street and is dominated by the Dolphin Hotel, which bears the name 'T Bland' (presumably its proprietor). During the Georgian period the many inns that clustered around St Mary's Church served as pit-stops for stage wagons, much as the George Hotel and The Swan in Bird Street focused on the coaching trade. Stage wagons were generally used for transporting goods, but it was possible to get a reasonably comfortable ride in one and they were cheaper than coaches. The Dolphin – first listed as a public house in 1818 – was one such pit-stop; other inns nearby included The George the Fourth (just out of shot on the right of the photograph) and The Goat's Head Tavern in Breadmarket Street. Next door to The Dolphin

are Bates' photography shop and the city seed store, while across the road there is a glimpse of a row of timber-framed houses that may have originally been built as shops. (Lichfield Heritage Collection)

THE DOLPHIN WAS demolished in 1912 and replaced the following year by the Edwardian classical building in this photograph (originally the Co-op and now a branch of menswear chain, Burton). Across the road, The George the Fourth is still going strong, keeping up a long tradition of inns on this site (a pub has stood here since at least 1750, and previous names for it have included The Old Goat's Head and The Old Golden Ball). According to John Shaw, part of The George the Fourth's premises were sold to the County Constabulary in 1851, but even while it operated as a police station (from rooms at the back of the building which still exist today), it continued to trade as a pub. The police moved next door into the Guildhall in 1889. The timber-framed shops on the south side of Bore Street, dating from the late sixteenth or early seventeenth century, still survive but their lower halves were cut away during the 1960s to create an arcaded walkway.

31

THE TUDOR OF LICHFIELD

THIS POSTCARD FROM about 1902 shows three of
the most important buildings on Bore Street. Far left
is the Guildhall – a Gothic structure built by Joseph
Potter Jnr of Lichfield in 1846-8, which incorporates
sections of an earlier date, including the City Prison.
In the middle is Donegal House – a townhouse built in
1730 for Lichfield merchant James Robinson. To the
right of that is The Tudor of Lichfield – dated 1510 and
known variously as Lichfield House, Boswell House and
the Tudor Café. The Tudor is particularly fascinating.
Anecdotal evidence suggests that a priest-hole is located
on the top floor – a puzzling feature for a building that
pre-dates Henry VIII's break with the Roman Catholic
Church by thirty years (it may have been added later,
of course, or the building may in fact be late sixteenth
century). The Tudor's cellar was used as a prison
during the Civil War, and a subterranean passage
is reputed to run between the cellar and Lichfield
Cathedral – presumably another relic of the Civil War.
(Author's collection)

MORE RECENTLY, THE Tudor of Lichfield has been a private residence, the offices of a coal merchant's, and a milliner's shop. It was requisitioned for the Army Pay Corps in 1910 and in 1920 became an antique shop. In 1935, Wilfred and Evelyn Burns-Mace and their son Jeffrey opened it as a teashop, and a teashop it remains today, though the cellars doubled as a public air-raid shelter in the Second World War. In 1975, its front threatened to slide into the street and the building was carefully restored (work which earned The Tudor a European Heritage Award). Comparing the two images, the densely patterned masonry in The Tudor's gables (c. 1902) has been toned down in the contemporary photograph, while the bottom storey has the appearance of a half-timbered building. At the far left of the photograph, The George the Fourth has been given a mock-Tudor makeover and we see the addition of the heads of King George V and Queen Mary on the front of the Guildhall, unveiled in 1910.

LICHFIELD GREENHILL BOWER

LICHFIELD IS FIERCELY protective of its traditions and one of its oldest is the Greenhill Bower, which was originally held on Whit Monday, and now takes place on Spring Bank Holiday Monday. Although its origins probably stretch back farther, the core elements seem to have originated with a twelfth-century royal statute that all men capable of bearing arms should be annually inspected by the magistrates (as there was no standing army, this was the only way of gauging England's fighting prowess in the event of a war). All able-bodied men were sent to the Commission of Arraye, and the musters were known as the Courtes of Arraye. Once assembled and inspected, the men would parade through the streets to a 'Bower House' at Greenhill, where they would receive free beef and wine. This photograph, taken by Sir J. Benjamin Stone, shows the Court of Arraye gathered outside the Guildhall on 1 June 1903. Amongst those pictured are the Mayor (George Haynes Esq.) and the Sheriff (J.T. Raby Esq.). This is a modern copy of the original photograph which was damaged in a flood in 1987. (Samuel Johnson Birthplace Museum)

34

THIS PHOTOGRAPH OF the Court of Arraye during a rainy Bower Day in 2011 demonstrates how little it has changed over the last 100 years. The people pictured in civic robes are, from left to right: Mike Williamson (mace-bearer), Dr Neville Brown (Sheriff), Brian Bacon (Mayor), Ken Knowles (sword-bearer), Janet Eagland (Deputy Mayor) and Alison Read (mace-bearer). Two reasons for the Bower's existence – its practical use as a mustering exercise and its religious symbolism as a celebration of Whitsun – have long since disappeared, but the event has successfully reinvented itself as a symbol of Lichfield's civic pride. Even as early as the nineteenth century, a local historian would complain that the Court of Arraye was 'an idle and useless ceremony adapted for the amusement of children', but nothing can dampen Lichfield's enthusiasm, it seems, for the ceremonials have grown to include the crowning of a Bower Queen and appearances from the band of the Brigade of Gurkhas. And although the alcohol is, sadly, no longer free, it does still flow all day. (Robert Yardley)

BORE STREET

ONE ASPECT OF Bore Street not in evidence today is its illustrious theatrical history. It is difficult to imagine the likes of Edmund Kean and Sarah Sidddons treading the boards here – but they did. In 1790, Lichfield had its first proper theatre (later called the Theatre Royal), built on Bore Street to a design by James Miller. It was, by all accounts, a Georgian architectural gem. Sadly, the building was demolished in the early 1870s, but another entertainment venue, St James's Hall, opened on the same site and can be seen about halfway down this postcard view (*c.* 1900) on the right-hand side of the street. By 1912, the entertainment business had shifted from stage to screen and St James's Hall was converted into various cinemas (the Palladium and the Lido) before coming full-circle in the 1950s and reopening as the David Garrick Theatre. The building in the foreground on the right is The Prince of Wales: an early nineteenth-century inn which traded under various names, including The Queen's Head and The Turf Tavern. (Author's collection)

THERE IS NO trace of Bore Street's theatrical heritage today, as the coming of television eventually saw off the David Garrick Theatre and it was replaced by a car accessories shop called Motormania. Finally, the building was demolished and a branch of Wilkinson's now stands in its place. The Prince of Wales is still on the right, and was until recently a tapas bar and club called The Feria (at the time of writing it is closed and boarded up). Lichfield has always experienced tensions between the preservation of its heritage and its requirements as a modern city, and the existence of the twentieth-century shops on the left are an echo of the bigger shopping developments that have taken place at the other end of Bore Street (note that, in this more sensitive area, the roof-lines have been kept low to avoid blocking the view of the spire of St Mary's). The entrance to the city arcade – built in the 1960s on the site of Garretts Bakery – was given a refurbishment in 1992, when it gained a mock-Tudor appearance.

THE FRIARY

THE PHOTOGRAPH FOR this postcard was probably taken about 1928 – a key moment in Lichfield's history because it marked the opening of the brand new Friary Road and school. This is undoubtedly the boldest development to have been undertaken in the city to date, the aim being to relieve the worsening problem of traffic congestion. Sadly, it also involved cutting the site of the city's ancient Friary in two. The Friary was founded in the 1230s by the Bishop of Coventry and Lichfield, Alexander de Stavensby (1224-38). It was burnt down in 1291 and then rebuilt again. In 1538, following the Dissolution of the Monasteries, large parts of it were demolished, but during the Restoration it came into the hands of Gregory Stonynge, who converted some of the old buildings into a large house. This fragment now forms one wing of the public library and Lichfield College, while the bulk of the structure – seen on the left of the

postcard – was built between 1921 and 1928 to a design by the County Education Committee Architect, G.C. Lowbridge. (Author's collection)

JOSEPH POTTER JNR'S Norman clock tower, built in 1863 for the Conduit Lands Trust (see p.28-9), still stands at the end of the road, though it is obscured by trees in this photograph. A curious addition to the Friary landscape is the Classical-style portico, made from sandstone and timber, erected across the road from Lowbridge's building in 1937. Sources differ on its origins; Howard Clayton claims it was taken from Shenstone Court – once the home of Sir Richard Cooper, demolished in 1937 – but others believe that it could have been made for the site. The public garden on the right of the contemporary photograph is actually the site of the former Friary church. When it was threatened with development in 1933 an excavation took place, revealing the layout of the original buildings. As a result the area became a Scheduled Ancient Monument, and the portico was erected to mark the former entrance to the complex. Slabs in the ground reveal the layout of the walls of the cloister and parts of the north wall of the nave.

VICTORIA HOSPITAL

THIS IS THE Victoria Hospital, designed by T.A. Pole of London and opened on land belonging to the Friary estate in 1933. The history of the hospital goes back much farther than this, however. The Victoria developed out of an older institution called the Lichfield Victoria Private Nursing Home, opened in 1899 at 15 Sandford Street for the treatment of the city's poor. The enterprise was reliant on subscriptions and donations, and was established using money from the city's funds for Queen Victoria's Jubilee celebrations of 1887 and 1897. The nursing home – itself formed from a merger between a nineteenth-century nursing institution and an invalids' kitchen – was the idea of Canon M.H. Scott, vicar of St Mary's (1878-94) and archdeacon of Stafford (1888-98). One of the two wards was named after him, and the other after Mary Slater of Haywood House, Bore Street, who left most of her residuary estate to the nursing association. The cost of the original Victoria Hospital – officially opened by Lady Cooper – was £2,030. (Lichfield Heritage Collection)

IN 1910, THE Lichfield Victoria Private Nursing Home's Sandford Street premises were enlarged at the cost of £1,377 and were re-opened by Lady Cooper under the revised name of the Lichfield Victoria Nursing Home and Cottage Hospital. But by 1920 a fund for an entirely new hospital had been started, and over a twelve-year period, £14,500 was raised towards the erection of a purpose-built structure. Colonel M.A. Swinfen Broun laid the foundation stone for the Victoria Hospital at the Friary: a site that was then surrounded by countryside. The hospital was officially opened in 1933 by Earl Harowby and in 1941 a twenty-four-bed maternity wing was added. A day room was opened in 1958, and a distinctive chair was designed by Dr Vaisey for patients to sit on while awaiting treatment. Yet by the mid-1990s the Victoria's future had become the subject of public debate. In 2005 the foundations of the Samuel Johnson Community Hospital were laid, and in 2007 the Victoria was closed and its site approved for a housing development. The road on which the houses now stand is named for hospital benefactress, Mary Slater.

ST JOHN STREET

ANCIENTLY KNOWN AS Lichfield Street or Culstrubbe Street, St John Street takes its name from its medieval almshouse, St John's Hospital, which was dedicated to St John the Baptist (see p.44). This postcard – published in the early 1900s by Lichfield publisher A.W. Mills – shows St John's House on the left: an impressive Greek Revival building with a façade that dates from around 1820 (the colonnade was inspired by the Tower of the Winds in Athens). As a result of twenty-first-century renovations to the building, hundreds of oyster shells were discovered in the garden, indicating that an inn may originally have stood here (a cheap and plentiful foodstuff, oysters were often sold in public houses). The business in question may in fact have been The Bear: a prominent coaching inn that ran services between North Wales and London during the Georgian period. A few doors down on the

left is the ivy-clad front of Marlborough House, built
around 1740 with a later porch consisting of pairs of
Tuscan columns. (Author's collection)

IT IS NOT known if St John's House incorporates parts of
The Bear inn or not, but the main structure does appear to
date from the mid to late eighteenth century. It underwent
a major renovation in the Regency period (when it gained
its fancy colonnade) and again in the Victorian period,
when the south wing and some stables were added. In
1849, a William East Holmes owned the house, followed
by iron merchant Frederick Simmonds in 1860 and in
1884 it was occupied by the Archdeacon John Allen,
who was Master of St John's Hospital. By 1902 it had
changed hands several times, eventually transferring to a
local colliery owner whose name was Peake (the building
was known as Peake House for a time). Around 1958,
St John's Preparatory School took over the property
and remained there for over thirty years. Following the
school's move to Longdon Green, Johann and Sarah Popp
purchased St John's House in 2003 and turned it into a
luxury B&B. Marlborough House, meanwhile, has been
converted into modern apartments.

ST JOHN'S HOSPITAL

ST JOHN'S HOSPITAL is one of two medieval almshouses still standing in Lichfield today (the other is Dr Milley's Hospital on Beacon Street). It was reputedly founded by the Bishop of Lichfield, Roger de Clinton, around 1135. Energetic and pragmatic, Clinton was determined to make Lichfield – then an isolated village – a place worthy of a cathedral. At the time, the process of demolishing the old Anglo-Saxon cathedral church of St Peter and replacing it with a new Romanesque building was probably underway, but it seems to have been Clinton who re-dedicated the cathedral to St Chad, and who added a defensive ditch and gates at various points around the city. The Hospital

of St John Baptist without the Barrs (to give it its proper title) was likely a waypoint for pilgrims visiting the Shrine of St Chad, who had arrived after the new gates were locked. This postcard was printed by Lichfield-based printers Lomax's Successors, some time between 1902 and 1906. (Author's collection)

MIRACULOUSLY, ST JOHN'S survived the Dissolution of the Monasteries, and the Civil War, and remains to this day a striking architectural landmark. The east range, with its stately line of chimneystacks, probably dates from 1495, when it was re-founded by Bishop William Smyth (1493-96) as an almshouse for thirteen elderly or infirm men within the Diocese of Lichfield. The adjoining chapel has undergone a great deal of change over the years; the eighteenth-century two-decker pulpit with tester and seats was removed, and, in 1829, the north aisle was added along with a chancel screen (now gone) and Victorian-style benches. The East Window – depicting Christ before the Mercian Cross – was the last major work by British artist John Piper (it was executed by Patrick Reyntiens in 1984). One of the most striking differences in the contemporary photograph is the addition to the West Wing, which was designed by Louis de Soissons and built between 1966 and 1967. Today, St John's continues its ancient life of worship and care, though is now open to married couples as well as to single men.

45

LICHFIELD CATHEDRAL
FROM STOWE

STOWE POOL (anciently Stowe Mere) separates Lichfield from the small settlement of Stowe. Dr Samuel Johnson had two good friends here – Jane Gastrell and her sister, Elizabeth Aston – each of whom owned a villa and gardens: Stowe Hill and Stowe House. They would have enjoyed an enviable view of the cathedral similar to the one in this postcard. James Boswell recalled an afternoon in 1776 when he was left sulking in Lichfield – 'a country town where I was an entire stranger' – while Johnson visited his friends at Stowe, but a dinner invitation from Mrs Gastrell soon followed and Boswell's spirits were restored. The white house in the photograph is Selwyn House: an eighteenth-century building known locally as Hate or Spite House. Legend has it that a third Aston sister, who remained unmarried, built it out of spite in order to spoil the view of the cathedral for her two married siblings. Even though the facts have since been disproved, the tale still lives on. (Author's collection)

STOWE POOL IS a popular place to capture Lichfield Cathedral at sunset. However, this is no ordinary view as the east end of the cathedral is covered in white plastic – a necessary step to protect the Lady Chapel during the restoration of the famous sixteenth-century Herkenrode windows. Designed and made in the Abbey of Herkenrode in Flanders (now Belgium), the glass panels were purchased for the cathedral in 1803 by Sir Brooke Boothby, to save them from the destruction of the Napoleonic Wars and to provide a replacement for Lichfield's medieval windows, lost during the Civil War. Despite surviving major religious and political upheavals they faced another danger in 2009 when the east end was found to be crumbling. Emergency funding from English Heritage and others allowed the panels to be removed and cleaned while the medieval masonry was repaired. The restoration process is expected to take at least five years, and currently the Lady Chapel windows have been replaced with clear glass, which will stay in place as a protective measure once the Herkenrode windows return around 2014.

JOHNSON'S WILLOW

THIS POSTCARD LOOKS towards the other end of Stowe Pool with Johnson's Willow on the left and St Chad's Church on the right. Like Shakespeare's mulberry tree in Stratford-upon-Avon, Johnson's Willow has mythical status in Lichfield. Dr Johnson is said to have visited it often because it stood by his father's parchment factory (a business that Michael Johnson ran from a cottage beside Stowe Pool). In 1781, a local physician, Dr Trevor Jones, drew up an account of the tree – reputedly a *Salix Russelliana* – at which time its entire height was 49ft. In 1819, Charles Edward Stringer made it 75ft high, but in 1829 or 1830 it was blown down entirely. According to one source it had experienced a fire – the fault of two boys named Barnes and Parker who had built a bonfire nearby – the sparks from which had ignited the hollow trunk. Some snuff boxes and other trinkets were made from the wood

and cuttings were taken and planted. Another 'legitimate successor' to Johnson's Willow was apparently blown down in 1881. (Samuel Johnson Birthplace Museum)

JOHNSON'S WILLOW IS barely discernable in this photograph due to the mass of foliage, but it still stands. It may not be *exactly* the same tree as in the old photograph, however, as the postcard seems to date from before 1938, while the current tree is said to have been planted in 1957. To the right of St Chad's Church is Stowe House: built in 1750 for Elizabeth Aston and later rented by the philosopher and eccentric Thomas Day. Day came to Lichfield in 1770 to consult Erasmus Darwin on a social experiment. As a disciple of the works of Rousseau, Day had adopted two foundling children, in whom he tried to instil virtues such as stoicism and bravery, with a view to moulding at least one of them into the perfect wife for himself. One of the girls, Sabrina – a pretty 13-year-old – lived with him briefly at Stowe House, but was later packed off to a boarding school in Sutton Coldfield when the project failed (Day apprenticed the other girl, Lucretia, to a milliner in London).

ST CHAD'S WELL

ST CHAD'S CHURCH is located at Stowe, about half a mile north-east of the cathedral, and was founded by Chad – Lichfield's first bishop – in AD 669. Chad chose this secluded, watery valley as a place to retire for reading and prayer, and here he built a church next to a well of spring water where he baptised his converts (the word 'Stowe' appears to mean 'holy place' or 'church'). According to Bede, the well had a stone at the bottom on which the saint stood naked and prayed; it soon became a place of pilgrimage and by the early eighteenth century the spring water had a reputation for easing sore eyes. In the late 1820s, the churchwardens of St Chad paid for the cleaning of the well, and in the 1830s the water supply was improved under the supervision of Dr James Rawson, a local physician and author of a tract attacking Lichfield's unhygienic pools (see p.18). Rawson also arranged for the octagonal stone structure to be erected over the well, as seen in this postcard, posted in 1927. (Author's collection)

ST CHAD'S WELL dried up in the early 1920s, and several modern interventions took place, including the fitting of a pump (which was inaugurated in a special ceremony held by the rector in 1923). The tradition of pilgrimage continued, with an annual Roman Catholic pilgrimage

taking place from 1922 into the 1930s, and an Anglican pilgrimage in 1926. Yet by the 1940s the well had become derelict. The octagonal building was removed in 1949 and an open structure with a tiled roof was constructed a few yards away (it is thought that the overgrown stones in the foreground of this picture mark the location of the nineteenth-century well). A vine was added to the roof in the 1980s and in 1995 the practice of well dressing was revived. At the time of writing, pilgrims are recreating a 90-mile walk from Chester to Lichfield which will conclude at St Chad's Well, where the Bishop of Lichfield, the Rt Revd Jonathan Gledhill, will unveil an interpretation panel containing a QR (Quick Response) code for smartphone users – almost certainly the first to be used on a pilgrimage route.

SAMUEL JOHNSON BIRTHPLACE MUSEUM

THIS PHOTOGRAPH – TAKEN by 'Varney' on 18 September 1900 – shows the house in which the lexicographer, essayist and wit, Samuel Johnson, was born in 1709. The house officially opened as a museum on 27 May 1901. John Gilbert (who is pictured at the door) donated the funds to purchase the Johnson Birthplace for the city. He was presented with the honorary Freedom of the City inside an ornate casket in thanks at a ceremony at the Guildhall – this photograph was taken directly afterwards. The *Staffordshire Advertiser* described the day as having the feel of a public holiday, with people lining the streets. At this time the building

still had tenants – a sign in the left window indicates that it was operating as a circulating library. The council served an eviction notice to a Miss Mallett a few days after this photograph was taken, in order to start work on preparing the museum. After the photographs were taken, the group moved on to a lunch hosted by Gilbert at the George Hotel. (Samuel Johnson Birthplace Museum)

THIS PLOT ON the corner of the Market Place was originally purchased by Samuel Johnson's father, who pulled down an old property in order to make way for this smart townhouse, completed in 1708. A bookseller and stationer, Michael Johnson no doubt saw the advantage of this central location, though, according to Boswell, he was still obliged to travel large distances between market days in order to make a living. The house remained in Samuel Johnson's possession until his death in 1784, and, although it was his intention to bequeath it to the city, it was sold for the sum of £235. The building changed hands many times during the nineteenth century – in 1817 it housed the *Lichfield Mercury* and later, the Dr Johnson Coffee House & Private Hotel. It became the Samuel Johnson Birthplace Museum in 1901 and has remained a museum ever since. The Birthplace now holds a collection of over 6,500 items relating to Johnson and his circle, including Johnson's silver bib-holder and a pair of his shoe buckles.

53

ANNUAL
JOHNSON SUPPER

THIS PICTURE FROM September 1928 shows members of the Johnson
Society posing with their churchwarden pipes at the Annual Supper in
Lichfield Guildhall. The tradition of marking Johnson's birthday was started
by Lichfield City Council in 1903, with the celebrations held annually on the
nearest convenient weekend to the birth-date (18 September). The event takes
place over several days and involves a service in Lichfield Cathedral and a
wreath-laying ceremony in the Market Square (see p.56). At the Annual Supper,
a new President of the Society is installed (in 1928 it was Johnson scholar
Robert White Chapman). Writing in 1936, J.W. Jackson describes the supper as
Georgian in style, 'with lighted candles, sanded floor, ale in earthenware mugs,
servitors in eighteenth-century dress, churchwarden pipes and the inevitable
punch'. On the menu were beef-steak puddings with kidneys, oysters and
mushrooms; a haunch of mutton; apple pie with cream 'mounted in the old
style' and toasted cheese. Note that the group is entirely male – women were
not permitted to attend until 1939. (Samuel Johnson Birthplace Museum)

THE INCLUSION OF women has not been the only change to the rules of the Johnson Society's Annual Birthday Supper. This photograph was taken in September 2006 – before the smoking ban had been fully introduced in Britain – and the tradition of smoking clay churchwarden pipes in the Guildhall is clearly still going strong. The ban came into force the following year and now guests migrate onto the street outside in order to smoke. The importance of the pipes should not be underestimated – to mark the tercentenary of Johnson's birth in 2009 the Society commissioned 300 commemorative churchwarden pipes, whose bowls were crafted into the likeness of the great lexicographer's face. The menu for the evening has remained similar since the event's inception and always includes the eminent man's favourites: home-made steak and kidney pudding, apple pie and custard, a cheeseboard and Bishop punch. Presidents continue to be chosen on an annual basis, not just from literature and academia but from all areas of public life including broadcasting, the press, the Church, industry, law and politics.

JOHNSON BIRTHDAY CELEBRATIONS

ANOTHER FACET OF the busy Johnson birthday activities is a civic ceremony that takes place annually in the Market Square. At noon on the Saturday following the launch of the celebrations, the Mayor, Sheriff and civic party, accompanied by the President and members of the Johnson Society, and staff and pupils from Johnson's old school, King Edward VI, process from the Guildhall to the Market Square and the Mayor places a laurel wreath on Johnson's statue. The choir sings a selection of hymns, including a setting of Johnson's Last Prayer, before the dignitaries return to the Guildhall to toast 'the immortal memory of Dr Johnson'. This photograph by John D. Short Jnr of Oxford, dated September 1966, is taken from behind the Johnson statue, facing the front of the Birthplace Museum

(here decorated with bunting and the Union Jack). The statue, sculpted by Richard Cockle Lucas in 1838, is a naturalistic depiction of Johnson seated in academic robes. We can just see the side of the pedestal, which contains scenes from the great man's life. (Samuel Johnson Birthplace Museum)

THIS PHOTOGRAPH SHOWS the wreath-laying ceremony in September 2011, on what would have been Johnson's 302nd birthday. The Mayor, Cllr Brian Bacon, delivered a short oration which concluded with the words: 'As Mayor of this Ancient and Loyal City it is my privilege to place on the statue of Dr Johnson a wreath to his immortal memory and as a tribute to his genius.' Two mace-bearers and the Town Crier stand to his left, along with pupils of King Edward VI's school. A similar wreath-laying event occurs every year in Uttoxeter Market Square on the following Monday. Johnson's father, Michael, once asked the young Samuel to man his stall in Uttoxeter because he was unwell, but the boy refused. As an adult, Johnson went to Uttoxeter where he stood in the rain on the same spot as an act of penance. Today, the event is marked by a wreath-laying on the conduit building, which contains a relief of Johnson's penance – a direct copy of Richard Cockle Lucas's relief on the pedestal of Johnson's statue in Lichfield.

MARKET STREET

THIS POSTCARD FROM around 1905 shows the top of Market Street, looking towards Bird Street, with the corner of the Johnson Birthplace Museum just visible on the left. On the right, nearest to the viewer, is the ornate eighteenth-century façade of a tobacconist shop owned by Samuel Wood, while next door we can clearly see the signage for Frisby's footwear business. About midway down on the left-hand side of the street stands The Scales public house (obscured by hanging signs in this picture). A pub since at least the mid-1600s, it was known as The Swan and Scales in the early nineteenth century and was used as weighing rooms for the Lichfield races before they moved to Whittington Heath (see p.94). On his return trips to Lichfield, Dr Johnson chose not to stay at The Scales, favouring instead an old-fashioned inn called The Three Crowns, which stood next door to his birthplace on Breadmarket Street. It was here that Boswell first saw oat ale and Staffordshire oatcakes, the latter 'soft like Yorkshire cake' and served at breakfast. (Author's collection)

WHAT IS STRIKING about this photograph is
the amount of street furniture that dominates
the view; however, the impressive façade of
Samuel Wood's shop (now City Jewellers) with
its typically Georgian multi-paned windows, has
been nicely preserved, as has the former Frisby's
(now clothing retailer Dorothy Perkins). Rather
surprisingly, the position of the window and steps
into Johnson's Birthplace on the Market Street
side has changed quite a bit (in addition to books,
it seems that Samuel Johnson's father sold last
dying speeches and quack medicines from this
building; a tract containing the dying words of one
Richard Cromwell, hanged at Lichfield for murder
in 1691, concludes with an incongruous advert
for the 'Queen of Hungaries Water', sold by 'Mich.
Johnson, bookseller'). Further down on the same
side of the street as Johnson's Birthplace Museum,
tucked out of sight just before The Scales pub, is a
very fine example of 1930s architecture, originally
built as a Burton's clothing store and now housing
Timpson and a toyshop. Its elegant Art Deco façade
can still be seen above shop level.

ST JOHN'S WHARF

KNOWN LOCALLY AS the 'Curly Wyrley', the Wyrley and Essington Canal was constructed to allow the transport of coal from the collieries at Wyrley Bank and Essington to Wolverhampton and Walsall, but it also carried limestone and other goods. An Act of Parliament was passed in 1792 which authorised the building of the canal, and in 1794 a supplementary Act was passed that enabled engineer William Pitt to extend the line to Brownhills, and then descend through thirty locks from Ogley Junction on the future Birmingham Canal Navigations (BCN) to Huddlesford Junction on the Coventry Canal near to Lichfield. The whole canal, including the extension, was completed by 1797 and by 1817 it is said that an average of 606 boats a year were unloading 10,302 tons of goods at six or more wharfs in Lichfield – the busiest two being either side of the London Road (St John's Wharf and Gallows Wharf). This photograph shows Lock 23 and the site of St John's Wharf after the canal had been abandoned in 1954. (LHCRT collection)

THINGS CHANGED FOR the Wyrley and Essington Canal after the Second World War; traffic declined and some branches were abandoned in 1954, including the length from Ogley Junction to Huddlesford Junction. Much of this section was drained and in-filled during the 1960s, though this view of the grassed-over canal basin of St John's Wharf shows that not all of the bridges were demolished. This isn't the end of the Wyrley and Essington's story, however. In 1988, the Lichfield & Hatherton Canals Restoration Trust (LHCRT) was formed to restore the Ogley section of the Wyrley and Essington Canal (re-named the Lichfield Canal) and also the Hatherton section through Cannock. Thanks to

donations, grants and the support of dedicated volunteers, the LHCRT has already made solid progress. Provided that funds can be raised, the section pictured here – the closest to the centre of Lichfield – will eventually become an 'attractive marina facility'. As its name suggests, Gallows Wharf, which stood on the other side of the London Road, was the site of the city's executions until 1810.

THE LICHFIELD CANAL

THIS SUPERB POSTCARD from around 1905 has been misattributed as the Wyrley and Essington Canal 'not far from where it passed under St John's Street', yet it never did pass under that street – the nearest it came to the centre of Lichfield was St John's Wharf (see p.60). This photograph was in fact taken by Fosseway Lane and shows Locks 16 and 17, which, according to D.A. Moore in *Restoring the Lichfield Canal*, 'formerly had large side pounds on the offside that extended right up to the hedge'. The side pounds increased the volume of water held in between each lock, a system that had dual benefits: it reduced the change in water level when boats locked in or out of the pound and it increased the speed with which the downstream chamber filled up. Re-excavating and re-lining the side pounds would be an expensive job, but these locks (part of a flight of five) would be an attractive feature if restored, providing a clear view of the cathedral spires. (Author's collection)

TODAY, THIS STRETCH of the old Wyrley and Essington Canal is a horse paddock on private farmland. A certain amount of detective work was needed in order to capture the view in the contemporary photograph, the main clues being the position of the spires on the horizon and the tell-tale white signal box, which still stands next to the level crossing on the mothballed South Staffordshire railway line to Walsall (see p.72). Canal brickwork is still visible in the fields and the undulations of the land where the side pounds stood are unmistakeable. The lock-keeper's cottage also still exists, though the cherry tree in the 'then' photograph was recently removed. In 2012, Lock 18 – beyond the cottage – was restored by the LHCRT but more funds are needed to rebuild this portion of the line. The old Fosseway Lane bridge was demolished and would have to be rebuilt, taking care (given a slight change in the alignment of the canal) to provide enough clearance for both the cottage and the old signal box.

GREENHILL

FOR CENTURIES GREENHILL operated as a market
place selling livestock. A pinfold, for impounding stray
animals, was recorded here as early as 1498, and
even in the twentieth century the area was still selling
cattle, sheep, pigs, wool and potatoes at a smithfield
in Church Street (on the site now occupied by Tesco),
with horses being sold on the first Friday of the month.
Greenhill has always had strong ties with the annual
Whitsun fair, which we know was taking place here
by the early fifteenth century. During the festivities,
dignitaries processed from the Guildhall to Greenhill,
where a 'Bower House' stood, and here the town crier
would announce the opening of the Court of Arraye
(see p.34). This postcard from around 1905 shows the
spire of St Michael's (see p.66) and below it, a drinking
fountain and cattle trough dedicated to that church's
rector: the Revd J.J. Serjeantson. The two-storey
building on the right is the old Bald Buck pub on its
original site, before it was demolished to make way for
the Birmingham Road. (Author's collection)

LOOKING AT THE current view, this is a picture of two distinct halves. On the right, the quaint cobbled street and its cottages have been swept away to make room for the busy junction with George Lane and Tamworth Street. But the buildings on the left-hand side of the road – two mid-eighteenth-century houses, followed by two late seventeenth or early eighteenth-century cottages with attics – are still reasonably intact. John Shaw identifies the cottages in the old photograph as David Fisher's butcher's shop and a small beer-house called the King William; today, they are still in commercial use. In the centre of the view, the Greenhill Medical Centre has replaced the row of cottages in front of St Michael's Church, but we can still see the spire and J.J. Serjeantson's memorial fountain. On the right is a branch of the hi-fi and TV retailer Richer Sounds, which took over when The Bald Buck Inn – opened here in 1957 as a replacement for the old pub of the same name – closed its doors in 2009.

ST MICHAEL'S CHURCH

THIS POSTCARD FROM the early 1900s shows St Michael's Church on its hilltop site at Greenhill, with children playing among the gravestones. The church was first recorded in 1190, but seems to stand on a much older religious site; a body found in a crouched position (known as a crouched burial: a type more common before the Conquest) has been found in its extensive graveyard – one of the largest in the country, and one of five ancient English burial grounds. It has been suggested that St Michael's was an early cemetery chapel which may have replaced a pagan sanctuary. Monuments of interest include a gravestone to John Brown, who sounded the trumpet for the 17th Lancers at the Charge of the Light Brigade on 25 October 1854, and the mausoleum of Thomas James Law (chancellor of the diocese 1821-54) and his wife, Lady Charlotte. The tomb was erected in 1864 and was originally surmounted by a clock, which was illuminated by gas for the benefit of those passing on their way to Trent Valley Station at night. (Author's collection)

IN 1906, THE spire was damaged in a storm and during the restoration work a new weathervane was erected. The tomb in the foreground, to the memory of the Adie family, seems to have lost its metal railings – probably as a result of the need for scrap metal during the Second World War (the old 'saddle-back' tomb behind it, dated 1674, has shared the same fate). Inside the church is a memorial to Samuel Johnson's father, Michael; his mother, Sarah; and his brother, Nathaniel (as St Mary's had no graveyard, most of its parishioners were buried at St Michael's). The tablet was placed in the floor of the nave in 1884 to mark the centenary of Samuel's death, and carries an inscription composed by Samuel for an earlier stone, which he ordered a few days before he died. The original stone was removed during repaving in the late 1790s. Unfortunately, much of St Michael's medieval fabric was lost during an extensive restoration in 1842-43 to a design by Thomas Johnson (no relation of the great lexicographer).

TRENT VALLEY ROAD

PUBLISHED IN 1927 by Tamworth Street newsagent W. Turner, this postcard shows the gatehouse to the Union Workhouse on the Trent Valley Road. The area around Greenhill has long been associated with workhouses. In 1740, St Michael's and St Chad's collaboratively ran a workhouse, but by 1780 it had moved premises and may have fallen victim to a fire that occurred in 1790. By 1811, St Michael's was single-handedly running a small workhouse in the former premises of The White Hart public house on Greenhill, which continued to operate until 1840, when Lichfield Union Workhouse opened. This building was a result of the passing of the Poor Law Act in 1834, which did away with parish workhouses and began to set up union workhouses with stricter controls. The competition to design the Union Workhouse was split between Thomas Johnson (who had restored St Michael's Church, see p.66) and the relatively unknown Scott and Moffatt.

Eventually the latter were chosen, helping to forge a successful ten-year partnership that saw the pair design over forty workhouses across Britain. (Author's collection)

THE 'SCOTT' OF Scott and Moffatt was in fact George Gilbert Scott, who returned to Lichfield eighteen years later to undertake an extensive restoration of the cathedral in the fashionable High Victorian Gothic style that he had helped to popularise (see p.88). Today, the gatehouse of the Union Workhouse (later St Michael's Hospital and now part of the Samuel Johnson Community Hospital) is the oldest remaining part of Scott and Moffatt's building – a red-brick Tudor-Gothic fantasy with battlements, a Georgian cupola and decorative blue-brick patterns known as diapers. Howard Clayton notes that the building cost £2,939 and all of the bricks were made on-site from the clay dug out in preparing the foundations, except for the 4,000 blue bricks used in the diapering. The workhouse accommodated 200 paupers of all ages, and there was wholesome food and proper sanitation (with water closets in every dormitory), though in return, inmates were expected to undertake such Victorian tasks as stone-breaking and oakum-picking (the latter – a preparation of tarred fibre – was also performed by the orphans in *Oliver Twist*).

LICHFIELD CITY STATION

WHEN THE SOUTH Staffordshire line was originally constructed, Lichfield City Station was located east of the current station, approached by a path that ran across Levett's Field near to the present Fire Station. Its architecture, by Edward Adams of London, was by all accounts modest and Tudor in style; the station was demolished in 1882 and the current one was built to accommodate the new Cross City Line. This photograph was taken by D.J. Norton on 30 June 1956, probably from the steps of Lichfield City No.1 Signal Box – the last remaining signal box at City, closed in October 1992 and subsequently demolished. Interestingly, it shows that the platform at that time extended right over the railway bridge that stands over St John's Street. The author of *Cross City Connections*, John Bassett, remembers being told that 20-30,000 people were coming through Lichfield City to the Bower at about the time that this photograph was

taken, and it took two days to sort out the used tickets and send them to Derby for auditing. The semaphore signals at Lichfield City were removed when the line was electrified (1991-3). (Mark Norton)

ONE OF LICHFIELD'S key industries in the later nineteenth century was brewing, and the building on the right of the old photograph, with the chimney, was a Lichfield Brewery Co. malthouse (the building bears the date 1858 and may have previously belonged to Beacon Street wine merchants and brewers, John and Arthur Griffith, see p.24). The building on the left is the City Flour Mill. The contemporary photograph shows a much lower view of the same scene from the end of the shortened platform. On the right, flats now stand on the site of the former goods yard, while part of the Lichfield Brewery Co.'s malthouse still survives just out of shot. On the left, the City Flour Mill (built in 1868 by J.C. Richardson) has long since been demolished. It was a working mill until 1962, when it was converted into a warehouse. In 1967 it was pulled down altogether to make way for the Kenning Motor Group's depot, although the adjoining house was preserved and is now occupied by a branch of the Co-operative Funeralcare.

71

LICHFIELD CITY STATION

LICHFIELD CITY STATION was for many years a major junction for two railways: the South Staffordshire line (Lichfield-Stourbridge via Walsall and Dudley, opened in 1850) and what is today the Cross City Line (opened to Lichfield in 1884). Today, the South Staffordshire line survives only as far as Brownhills as the mothballed, single track Anglesea branch, but in 1956 it was a major route serving the Black Country. Semaphore signal gantries at Lichfield City controlled the junction, as well as access to the extensive goods sidings at Lichfield City itself. This picture, taken by D.J. Norton on 30 June 1956, shows an unidentified Stanier 8F class locomotive hauling a mineral train, passing through Lichfield City station. To the left of the locomotive, at the end of the platform, is the Lichfield City No.2 signal box; taken out of use in November 1973 and subsequently demolished. Lichfield City station itself had an extensive goods yard, including private sidings

serving the City Brewery Co., which can be seen to the right of the picture, with large numbers of mineral wagons awaiting shunting. (Mark Norton)

SINCE THE END of regular freight traffic on the former South Staffordshire line in 2001, Lichfield City station is now used almost exclusively by passenger trains. The Cross City Line from Redditch via Birmingham New Street to Lichfield Trent Valley was electrified in 1993, at which time the track layout at Lichfield City was radically simplified, with almost all remaining sidings being removed. The former goods yard has been cleared and is now the site of the City Wharf housing development; the former goods shed (visible behind the train to the left of the picture) remains but is now owned by a tool and equipment hire firm. Although the No.2 signal box has been demolished, the main station building and canopy, built by the London & North Western Railway in 1882, survive. Since the age of steam, the Cross City Line has acted as a diversionary route for long-distance passenger services on Sundays (when other main routes into Birmingham are closed for engineering work), and on this Sunday in 2011, two Cross Country Trains Voyager DMUs were captured en route for Edinburgh and the West Country, respectively.

BAKERS LANE
SHOPPING PRECINCT

DESIGNED BY SHINGLER & Risdon of London, this shopping precinct was built in the early 1960s following the demolition of Victorian slums in Bakers Lane (an area quaintly known as Peas Porridge Lane during the seventeenth century). Shingler & Risdon were at the forefront of the architectural boom of the 1960s, and despite the fact that their modernist shopping centre was a bold move for a city with a conservative approach to architecture, it made sense to site it in Bakers Lane – one of the city centre's least sensitive areas in terms of heritage. Yet by 1980 this breezy optimism had turned to frustration as locals complained about the lack of a department store and worried that Lichfield was not moving with the times. By the mid-1990s Shingler & Risdon's design was showing its age, but a London company, St Mary's Property Investments, redeveloped the site and the Three Spires Shopping Centre was opened in 1995-6. In 2000, the same company redeveloped the Levetts Square area (pictured right). (Lichfield Heritage Collection)

HERE IS THE Three Spires shopping centre, seen from Garrick Square (above), with the side of the Lichfield Garrick Theatre just visible on the right. Designed by Alan Short, the Garrick stands on the site of the old Civic Hall, which was drastically re-modelled in 2002-3 to provide Lichfield with a contemporary mid-sized entertainment venue. The Three Spires Shopping Centre is currently owned by Orchard Street Investment

Management and Jones Lang LaSalle, but in today's challenging financial climate the centre is facing additional competition from S. Harrison Developments, which, at the time of writing, wants to build a new £100m shopping centre, Friarsgate, on the land behind the Garrick Theatre. The project has received much attention locally, reviving old conflicts between the desire to preserve Lichfield's heritage and the need to serve a growing population. Earlier plans for a high-rise hotel on the site of Lichfield's bus station have been scrapped, yet, despite attempts to yoke together Friarsgate and the Three Spires in a unified design, the Friarsgate development could threaten the future of the Three Spires Shopping Centre in years to come.

TAMWORTH STREET

THIS IS THE shop of Lichfield butcher Quantrill (established 1870, later Quantrills) on the corner of Bakers Lane before it was demolished in 1962/3 to make way for a shopping precinct. This building was first occupied by Quantrill in 1889, but it was the property of the Suffolk family from a least 1850. In the late eighteenth century the whole area from Bore Street to the north side of the market place was connected with the cattle trade, so it is unsurprising to find that, prior to Quantrill's ownership, the property is occupied by 'butcher and cattle dealer' Thomas Suffolk. On the right of the photograph is The Old Crown, a large

inn with a long history, having been recorded by Snape on his 1781 map of Lichfield. Curiously, Snape marked two Old Crowns – this one on the corner of Bakers Lane and Bore Street and another in Tamworth Street, near to the junction with Conduit Street; it is not known if the two businesses were connected in any way. (Lichfield Heritage Collection)

THE SCENE TODAY does not look incredibly different, apart from the absence of Quantrill's shop. What might not be immediately obvious is that The Old Crown – now housing an empty shop and a branch of Boots Opticians – has been completely rebuilt since its days as a pub, the building having dramatically fallen down one night shortly after it was converted into retail units. On the left in both photographs is Boots the Chemist, built in 1908 to a design influenced by the Arts and Crafts movement. With its gabled M-shaped roof and its large sheet-glass windows set behind a ground-floor timber loggia, it is one of Lichfield's finer examples of mock-Tudor architecture; close inspection of the first floor reveals some relief panels depicting medieval scenes, including a male figure playing a pipe, an owl within a canopy of leaves, and a beehive emblem with three bees. One of the city's conduits stood close to this spot at the junction between Bore Street and Conduit Street from around 1482 until the turn of the nineteenth century.

MARKET PLACE
AND DAM STREET

THIS POSTCARD, SHOWING the corner of Market Street and
Dam Street, appears to date from the 1920s when the Market
Place served as a departure point for buses to Birmingham and
Tamworth. The building nearest to the viewer on the right is
The Malt Shovel Inn. First listed in 1592, it was always popular
with waggoners and market traders. The elegant building
with the finial, just peeping through the trees on the left-hand
side of the postcard, is the premises of F.J. Long & Son. The
photographer is standing in Conduit Street – anciently called
Butcher Row. Charles Stringer, writing in 1819, says that
every house in Butcher Row was furnished with a 'shambles'
(butcher's slaughterhouse), which is hardly surprising when
you consider that meat from the cattle market at Greenhill would
have naturally found its way into the Market Place via this street.
One of the buildings, just out of sight on the right, still bears
two ornamental bovine heads on the front of what was formerly
Hall's butchers shop. (Author's collection)

THE CONTEMPORARY VIEW is a much less cluttered scene. On the right, the former Malt Shovel has disappeared, having closed in 1969, and – following a mock-Tudor makeover in 1972 – the building became a branch of electrical goods retailer, Currys (it later changed to Dixons and back to Currys again, and at the time of writing stands empty). It was in the early 1970s that the former premises of F.J. Long & Son also received a radical transformation, having been bought by The Midland Bank (it is now a branch of HSBC). In front of the bank, and much more visible – thanks to the absence of the bus stop – is the bronze statue of James Boswell by Percy Hetherington Fitzgerald, presented to the city by the sculptor in 1908. It shows Samuel Johnson's biographer in eighteenth-century dress with a notebook under his arm and a sword by his side. The top of the pedestal contains medallions of five of Boswell's friends, while underneath, Boswell and Johnson's friendship is celebrated in a series of sculptural vignettes.

QUONIANS LANE

AS WITH OTHER ancient Lichfield street names, there are conflicting theories about the origin of Quonians (sometimes Quoniams) Lane. Some think it could have derived from the Latin *quoniam*, whereas others believe it originates from the corruption of the family name Conyngham (Conyngham or Cunnigham means 'King's house' and old documents show this area to have been recorded as King's Meadow Land). Although a picturesque backwater for many centuries, Quonians Lane was probably intended for greater things in the Middle Ages when Lichfield's street plan was first developed. A glance at the map shows that Lichfield's

city centre was originally laid out like a ladder, with St John Street/Bird Street and Tamworth Street/Dam Street standing in parallel to each other, while Frog Lane, Wade Street, Bore Street and Market Street are positioned horizontally like rungs. The alignment of Quonians Lane with the alleyway alongside the George Hotel (anciently called Cock Lane) suggests that it was supposed to be another rung on the ladder, though the streets do not appear ever to have been joined up. (Lichfield Heritage Collection)

THE STREET HAS been very well preserved, probably because of two important historical connections. The first is Dr Johnson, who was educated at the Dame School run by Ann Oliver on the corner of Dam Street and Quonians Lane (early timbers from this building are supposed to survive). The other is the premises of stonemason Robert Bridgeman (see pp.14-15), which can be seen in both of these pictures. Bridgeman first came to Lichfield in 1877 to work on the cathedral, soon establishing his own business just off Dam Street by Minster Pool. By 1882 he had moved to Quonians Lane, where his business flourished. Having been passed down to successive members of the Bridgeman family it was eventually sold to Cannock-based firm Linfords in 1968, and at the time of writing is still operating as Linford Bridgeman. According to Charles Stringer, a large subterranean arched passage of stone, several feet beneath the surface, has been traced from the middle of Quonians Lane to a considerable distance under the houses on the west side of Dam Street, though its purpose is a mystery.

LICHFIELD THEOLOGICAL COLLEGE

THIS ATMOSPHERIC POSTCARD, posted to a Yorkshire vicarage around 1917, shows Lichfield Theological College peeping through the trees and the iron railings dividing Dam Street from Minster Pool. A site in the Close (anciently a residence for chantry priests) was acquired by the Theological College in 1872. It had originally comprised chambers around a central courtyard with a buttery at its west end, but was by then a series of separate houses. The Principal was installed in one of these houses (formerly owned by Richard Wright, who used it to display objects from the museum of his grandfather, Richard Greene) and a library and student rooms were added to the range. At one end of the lecture room a small apse was thrown out to serve as a chapel. Bishop Selwyn (1867-78), who was a great supporter of the scheme, opened the building with a special service in 1873, which was attended by the choristers and several of the clergy of the cathedral. A chapel was added in 1885. (Author's collection)

AFTER THE CLOSURE of the Theological College in 1972, it was let to the Trustees of St John's Hospital (see p.44), who demolished it and built in its place an almshouse called St John's within the Close. Part of the chapel still stands, however, and in 1980 was converted into a social centre known as the Refectory. The railings in the foreground of the old photograph were probably removed as a result of the scrap-metal drive in the Second World War. In 2008, Speakers' Corner Trust began a consultation with civic and community leaders to create an area in the city where open-air public speaking, debate and discussion would be encouraged. A bronze plaque was unveiled at this location beside Minster Pool in 2009 (the year of Dr Samuel Johnson's tercentenary), and has since been embellished with a handrail and a small stone podium containing the following words by Johnson: 'In order that all men may be taught to speak truth, it is necessary that all likewise should learn to hear it.'

CATHEDRAL CLOSE

JUDGING FROM THE similarity of these two views, the
Close has not undergone many changes since the beginning
of twentieth century, yet the years between the Civil War
and the Victorian era brought major upheavals. The Close
was the target of both bombardment and vandalism during
the Civil War, which led to the destruction of almost all
of the houses on the south side (which had been within
range of mortar-fire from across Minster Pool), while the
houses of the Dean and Chapter, Precentor and Bishop
were 'exceedingly ruined and demolished'. By 1660,
there were no less than six alehouses in operation here,
and pigs rooted amongst the grass. At the Restoration,
Bishop Hacket (1661-70) and others began the task of
repairing the damage; by the 1720s, Daniel Defoe – visiting
Lichfield on his tour of Great Britain – was able to observe:
'There are in the Close, besides the houses of the clergy
residentiaries, a great many very well-built houses, and
well inhabited too; which makes Lichfield a place of good
conversation and good company.' (Author's collection)

AS HINTED BY Defoe, the Close's reputation as a centre of polite society partly stemmed from the fact that Lichfield's bishops and many of its canons were reluctant to reside there, so the grander houses, such as the Bishop's Palace, were let to wealthy and fashionable tenants (see pp.86). By the late eighteenth century an avenue of trees known as Dean's Walk (much favoured by Dr Johnson on his return visits to Lichfield) had been planted along the north and east sides of the Close. Selwyn House, which stands in the west ditch (see p.64), was built in 1780, and the entrance to the Close from Beacon Street was widened in 1800 to make way for Newton's College (see p.8). The houses that we see today, though substantially rebuilt in the eighteenth century, probably echo the original medieval layout of the Close, and, despite the destruction of the Civil War, a few medieval buildings have survived, most notably an impressive range of timber-framed buildings, tucked away in the north and south courtyards of Vicars' Close (see pp.90-93).

THE BISHOP'S PALACE

THE BISHOP'S PALACE was built in 1687-8, to a design by Edward Pierce, one of Wren's masons. It stands on the site of a former palace, erected for Bishop Walter de Langton (1296-1321) and destroyed during the Civil War. The remains of the old palace had been used as a quarry when Bishop Hacket (1661-70) renovated a house on the south side of the Close. Hacket was old yet still energetic when he came to Lichfield, overseeing the rebuilding of both the cathedral and the Close, but this additional damage to the shell of Langton's palace was seized upon by his successor, Bishop Wood (1671-92), who attempted to sue Hacket's son and executor, Sir Andrew Hacket, for compensation. One of Lichfield's worst Bishops, Wood held a long enmity towards his predecessor. Hacket had excommunicated Wood during the latter's

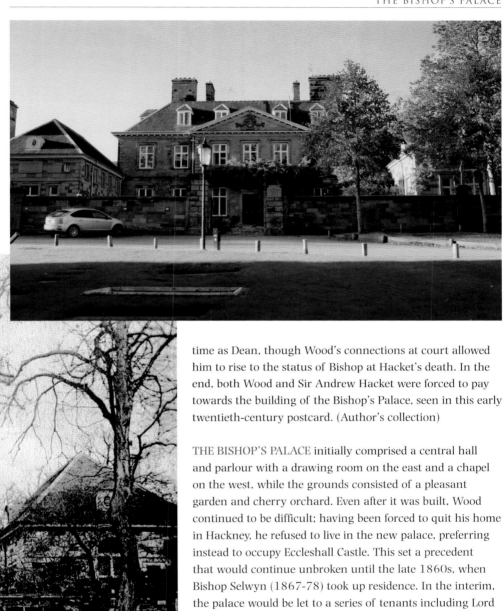

time as Dean, though Wood's connections at court allowed him to rise to the status of Bishop at Hacket's death. In the end, both Wood and Sir Andrew Hacket were forced to pay towards the building of the Bishop's Palace, seen in this early twentieth-century postcard. (Author's collection)

THE BISHOP'S PALACE initially comprised a central hall and parlour with a drawing room on the east and a chapel on the west, while the grounds consisted of a pleasant garden and cherry orchard. Even after it was built, Wood continued to be difficult; having been forced to quit his home in Hackney, he refused to live in the new palace, preferring instead to occupy Eccleshall Castle. This set a precedent that would continue unbroken until the late 1860s, when Bishop Selwyn (1867-78) took up residence. In the interim, the palace would be let to a series of tenants including Lord Stanhope, later Earl, of Chesterfield; Gilbert Walmisley (the Bishop's registrar) and the Revd Thomas Seward, whose daughter, the poetess and biographer Anna Seward, fondly referred to it as 'our pleasant home'. The projecting wings to the left and right of the building – praised by architectural historian Nikolaus Pevsner as 'amazingly sensitively done' – were added by Selwyn in 1869. Today the Bishop's Palace is used by Lichfield Cathedral School.

LICHFIELD CATHEDRAL, WEST FRONT

THIS POSTCARD SHOWS one of Lichfield's chief glories: the west front of the cathedral. In the thirteenth century the west front's decoration was said to have consisted of 113 statues, but the majority of these were destroyed during the Civil War. Following Bishop Hacket's structural restoration of the cathedral very little work was done on it, so that by 1820 the stonework was in poor condition. Dean Woodhouse (1807-33) swept the remains of the medieval statues away (with the exception of five at the top of the north-west tower) and encased the whole front in Roman cement. It was Sir George Gilbert Scott (see p.69) – during his forty-year restoration job on the cathedral – who designed the façade that we see today. Most of the west front figures were carved by local firm Bridgeman (see p.81), although two women were involved: London sculptress Miss M. Grant carved the figures around the central doorway (including Christ), while Princess Louise carved the likeness of her mother, Queen Victoria. (Author's collection)

HERE IS THE same view during the Lichfield Festival Market, which is held every year in July. One of the interesting features of the old photograph is the stone-encased water pump on the corner of the Cathedral Green, which is today almost completely hidden by bushes. This pump was installed in 1786, as a replacement for an older conduit head that had become an eyesore. The old conduit had been surmounted by a cross and was known as 'Moses' (a reference to the prophet's miracle in the desert of Zin, when he struck a rock twice with his rod, causing water to flow). Unfortunately, the water supply to the new reservoir soon proved inadequate and in 1803 another conduit was built in the south-west corner of the garden of No. 15, the Close. This water source later failed too, but by 1876 the Close was connected to the city's water supply, leaving the conduit in the garden of No. 15 free to be used as a refreshment kiosk. Along with the stone pump, the former conduit-kiosk still stands today.

VICARS' CLOSE (UPPER COURTYARD)

IN 1315, BISHOP Langton (1296-1321) gave the Vicars Choral some land at the west end of the Close and they built their houses around two courtyards with a common hall. This postcard shows the entrance to the upper courtyard, known by the 1980s as Vicars' Close, and, on the corner, a large timber-framed fifteenth-century house. Vicars' Close is one of the city's many architectural jewels, rivalled only by the Vicars' Close at Wells. It seems incredible that, of the twenty houses belonging to the Vicars Choral in 1649, only the common hall in the upper courtyard, and two houses in the lower courtyard – near to the west gate – were heavily damaged in the Civil War (the houses in the lower courtyard stand behind what is now the

Erasmus Darwin House, see p.92). The common hall was taken down and rebuilt in brick in 1756, with an oriel window facing Beacon Street. It was used for public assemblies until the late eighteenth century, but was later split and remodelled into flats. (Author's collection)

AS WITH THE Tudor of Lichfield (see p.32) one obvious difference is the removal of the patterned masonry (probably Victorian embellishment) on three of the houses in this photograph. Today, the buildings in Vicars' Close are principally occupied by people associated with the cathedral community. Many of the houses of the Vicars Choral have been extensively remodelled over the centuries, but the most complete examples of original medieval architecture can be seen along the north side of the upper courtyard, a 'pleasant backwater' according to Nikolaus Pevsner, 'reached through a narrow gangway through a house. There is a lawn in the middle and a tree, and [the] houses are timber-framed on the north and east'. Number 5, which adjoins the Vicars' common hall, was rebuilt in 1764, while Nos 8 and 9 were restored in 1990. This view not only shows the entrance to Vicars' Close, but also part of a Victorian red-brick building on the right, owned by Lichfield Cathedral School (formerly St Chad's School). Part of this building was damaged by fire in 2012.

VICARS' CLOSE (LOWER COURTYARD)

THIS POSTCARD SHOWS the narrow passage between the houses of the lower courtyard of Vicars' Close, leading into the Cathedral Close. Unlike the houses in the upper courtyard, which have a 'college-style' arrangement (i.e. facing inwards around a courtyard), these were remodelled in the early eighteenth century to face outwards towards the cathedral and the approach road from Beacon Street. The bases of the houses on the south side of the lower courtyard date from 1474, when they were rebuilt by Dean Heywood, but by 1732 they would have looked much as they do today (two houses at the west end of the range, now Nos 2 and 3 the Close, were heightened and given fronts of five bays). The reason for the remodelling was apparently not destruction during the Civil War, since the houses were still thought to be in good order by the early eighteenth century; it may simply have been an influx of wealthy tenants who wished to update the look of the properties. (Author's collection)

ONE WELL-TO-DO tenant who lived here was Erasmus Darwin: physician, Enlightenment thinker and grandfather of Charles Darwin. Following his marriage in 1757, he leased a timber-framed house that stood partly on land known in the eighteenth century as Dovehouse; it was built over medieval cellars on the west side of the lower courtyard and communicated with the Vicars' common hall in the upper courtyard (which he would later use as his treatment rooms). Like the other occupants of the lower courtyard, he converted the original timber-framed building into a modern brick structure facing out towards Beacon Street, with grand Venetian windows and a bridge across the remains of the Close's defensive ditch. In 1999, the building – now known as Erasmus Darwin House – was restored and turned into a museum devoted to Darwin's work, while the courtyard area became a herb garden with a resident rabbit (Darwin himself kept rabbits). The only change between these two photographs appears to be the substitution of wheelie bins for wooden barrels!

GRANDSTAND, LICHFIELD RACECOURSE

THIS POSTCARD, POSTED in 1906 by a convalescent soldier at Whittington Heath Barracks, shows an interesting nineteenth-century building with strong Lichfield connections. From 1702, Whittington Heath was the location of Lichfield's horse races, with meetings held here every September by the early 1740s. The first grandstand was erected by public subscription in 1773, followed by a larger one (donated by Lord Paget) in 1803. Between 1840 and 1875 a new brick grandstand – pictured here – was built by the main road between Tamworth and Lichfield. By this point the races were already on the decline, yet the Heath's use as a military base was on the rise. The barracks were built between 1877 and 1881 and the Staffordshire Regiment took up residence, turning the old grandstand into a Soldiers' Home. Miss M. Allen was the first Lady Superintendent, but the best remembered was Mrs Key, who held the post for thirty years. Could she be the lady with the bicycle in this photograph? (Author's collection)

THE GRANDSTAND CONTINUED to be used as a Soldiers' Home until 1957, when Whittington Golf Club acquired it from the War Office for use as a clubhouse. The introduction of golf to Whittington Heath happened at the instigation of a military man, Colonel George Simon, who, in 1886, requested permission from his Commanding Officer to create a nine-hole course as a morale-boosting treat for troops stationed at the barracks. It remained a military club for a few years, but civilians were eventually admitted too. In 1927 the course was extended to eighteen holes, but the advent of the Second World War meant that Whittington Heath was again put to military use – this time by the US Army. Its civilian members having purchased it from the military in 1994, Whittington Heath continues to be a popular golf club, though in 2012 its future is far from certain. At the time of writing, a new high-speed rail link (HS2) between London and Birmingham is set to cut through the course, leaving this historic clubhouse under threat of demolition.

BIBLIOGRAPHY

BOOKS

Bassett, John, *Cross City Connections*, Brewin Books, Warwickshire, 1990

Beresford, William, *Diocesan Histories: Lichfield*, Society for Promoting Christian Knowledge, London, 1883

Clayton, Howard, *Loyal and Ancient City: Lichfield in the Civil Wars*, Abbotsford Publishing, Lichfield, 1987

Clayton, Howard, *Mr Lomax's Lichfield*, Howard Clayton, Lichfield, 1991

Clayton, Howard, *Cathedral City: A Look at Victorian Lichfield*, Abbotsford Publishing, Lichfield, 1992

Clayton, Howard, and Simmons, Kathleen, *The Lily-White Swann: A History of the Swan Hotel Lichfield*, Abbotsford Publishing, Lichfield, 1998

Clayton, Howard, *Coaching City: A Glimpse of Georgian Lichfield*, Abbotsford Publishing, Lichfield, 2009

Clayton, Howard and Simmons, Kathleen, *The Spirit of Lichfield: The 20th Century in Photographs*, Landmark Publishing Ltd, Ashbourne, 2000

Clayton, Howard and Simmons, Kathleen, *Lichfield (Britain in Old Photographs)*, The History Press, Stroud, 2009

Defoe, Daniel, *A Tour Through the Whole Island of Great Britain*, Penguin Classics, London, 1978

Elrington, C.R. (ed.), *The Victoria History of the Counties of England*, Volume XIV: Lichfield, Oxford University Press, Oxford, 1990

Essery, R.J., *D.J. Norton's Pictorial Survey of Railways in the West Midlands, Part One*, Wild Swan Publications Ltd, Didcot, 2008

Gallagher, J.P., *Trades of a City: Lichfield Shops and Residents from 1850*, The Lichfield Press, Lichfield, 2006

Harper, Rob, *Lichfield City Conservation Area Document*, Lichfield District Council, Lichfield, 1997

Hewitt, John, *Handbook for the City of Lichfield and its Neighbourhood*, Alfred Charles Lomax, Lichfield, 1874

Holt, Tonie and Valmai, *Picture Postcards of the Golden Age: A Collector's Guide*, Postcard Publishing Company, London, 1978

Hopkins, Mary Alden, *Dr Johnson's Lichfield*, Peter Owen Ltd, London, 1956

Hutchinson, Mary, Croot, Ingrid and Sadowski, Anna, *This Won't Hurt: A History of the Hospitals of Lichfield*, Lichfield Hospitals History Group, Lichfield, 2010

Jackson, J.W., *Historical Incidents in and Around Lichfield and its Ancient Charities*, The Lichfield Mercury Ltd Press, Lichfield, 1936

James, Ralph, *Lichfield Then and Now*, Lichfield Press, 1988

Lewis, R.A., *Lichfield Maps (Local History Source Book)*, Staffordshire County Council Education Department, 1970

Lewis, Roy, *Lichfield on Old Picture Postcards (Yesterday's Staffordshire)*, Reflections of a Bygone Age, Nottingham, 1994

Martin, Stapleton, *Anna Seward and Classic Lichfield*, Deighton and Co., Worcester, 1909

Mee, Arthur, *Staffordshire: Beauty and the Black Country*, Hodder and Stoughton Ltd, London, 1948

Moore, D.A., *Restoring the Lichfield Canal*, The Lichfield and Hatherton Canal Restoration Trust, Lichfield, 1992

Noszlopy, George T. and Waterhouse, Fiona, *Public Sculpture of Staffordshire and the Black Country*, Liverpool University Press, Liverpool, 2005

Pevsner, Nikolaus, *Staffordshire*, Penguin Books Ltd, Harmondsworth, 1975

Poulton-Smith, Anthony, *South Staffordshire Street Names*, Amberley Publishing, Stroud, 2009

Rawson, James, *An Enquiry into the History and Influence of the Lichfield Waters*, Lomax, Lichfield, 1815

Shaw, John, *The Old Pubs of Lichfield*, George Lane Publishing, Lichfield, 2001

Stringer, Charles Edward, *A Short Account of the Ancient and Modern State of the City and Close of Lichfield*, T.G. Lomax, Lichfield, 1819

Upton, Chris, *A History of Lichfield*, Phillimore & Co. Ltd, Chichester, 2001

Wilkinson, Roger and Burgess, John E., *Look at Lichfield*, James Redshaw Ltd, Lichfield, 1976

Williams, Roger and Wilkes, Alan, *St John's Hospital Lichfield*, St John's Hospital, Lichfield

WEBSITE

Gomez, Kate, *Lichfield Lore* (blog), www.lichfieldlore.co.uk